by Simon Gaspard

HOUGHTON MIFFLIN BOSTON

PHOTOGRAPHY CREDITS: Cover © Gideon Mendel/Corbis; Toc © Martin Harvey/Alamy; 2 © Image100/Corbis; 3 © OnAsia/JupiterImages; 4 © Gideon Mendel/Corbis; 5 © Martin Harvey/Alamy; 6 © Despotovic Dusko/Corbis

Printed in China

ISBN-13: 978-0-547-01821-8
ISBN-10: 0-547-01821-5

12 13 14 15 0940 17 16 15 14
4500496268

We can see a seal.

We can see a turtle.

We can see a shark.

We can see a crab.

We can see penguins!

Responding

TARGET SKILL **Details** This book is about an aquarium. What animals live in the aquarium?

Write About It

Text to World Draw a picture of an animal you can see at an aquarium. Label your picture. Then tell details about your picture.

a

TARGET SKILL **Details** Tell important details about a topic.

TARGET STRATEGY **Visualize**

Picture what is happening as you read.

GENRE **Informational text** gives facts about a topic.